P9-CDY-291

DO ONE THING EVERY DAY THAT MAKES YOU HAPPY

This journal of joy belongs to:

_____

"WHAT MAKES YOU HAPPIEST?"

THIS IS ONE OF ABOUT

thirty questions from a confession album popular in France at the end of the nineteenth century and revived a century later as the Proust Questionnaire in *Vanity Fair* magazine. Happiness is a theme that has inspired varied thoughts throughout time—from Psalm 147 in the Bible ("a joyful and pleasant thing it is to be thankful") to the words of Ellen DeGeneres ("I don't know how happiness could get any more perfect, but I think it would involve more puppies").

Do One Thing Every Day That Makes You Happy offers a journey to discover what brings you the greatest joy. Your guides are the most thoughtful and thought-provoking words of poets, artists, entertainers, novelists, scientists, politicians, and philosophers, from the past and from today. Prompts, based on these quotations, will lead you to look inside and outside of yourself and to act on ideas small and large, in order to mine the potential for joy in every day.

In this journal you will have opportunities to identify your own simple "Delights of the Day," to rank your top five favorites in various categories, and to draw an expression on your own emoji face. There are pages on which to record happy holidays (both the calendar kind and your own personal version), gifts given and received, and the smiles and laughs that brighten your life and the lives of others. You will reflect on the sources of joy in your life—love, art, nature, food, friendship, kindness, learning, action, and work.

Mark your starting level of happiness on the happiness meter here, today. You will then find happiness charts along the way to use as checkpoints and to reorient you if you get off track. Finally, after moving in, out, and around the quotes and exercises, you will reach another meter at the end of the book. There you can gauge the impact of your year's journey toward a personal definition of delight. Go through the pages in order or jump around as you please; just get ready to be happy.

DATE: __/__/__

The measure of my happiness today:

DATE: __/__/__

HAPPY HOLIDAY!

What made this New Year's Eve happy:

_____

_____

_____

New Year's Day is every man's birthday.

Charles Lamb

How I started a happy new year:

_____

_____

_____

Pleasure is the object, duty, and the goal of all rational creatures.

Voltaire

My goal for pleasure today:

_____

_____

_____

Find me playing till sunrise for 50 cents and a sandwich.

Muddy Waters

What I would be delighted to do all night for 50 cents and a sandwich:

_____

_____

_____

There is only one
to love and

DATE: __/__/__

I LOVE:

happiness in life, be loved. ▶ George Sand

DATE: __/__/__

LOVES ME.

DATE: __/__/__

I have found that most people are about as happy as they make up their minds to be.

Abraham Lincoln

Today I made up my mind to be:

[ ] content   [ ] pleased

[ ] glad   [ ] cheerful

[ ] delighted   [ ] gleeful

[ ] thrilled   [ ] jubilant

[ ] elated   [ ] ecstatic

OPTIMISM IS A KIND OF HEART STIMULANT— THE DIGITALIS OF FAILURE.

Elbert Hubbard

How optimism stimulated my heart today:

_____

_____

_____

DATE: __/__/__

The art of being happy lies in the power of extracting happiness from common things.

Henry Ward Beecher

A common thing that made me happy today:

_____

_____

_____

Nothing is more pleasant to the eye than green grass kept finely shorn.

Francis Bacon

Nothing is more pleasant to my eye than:

_____

_____

_____

DATE: __/__/__

WORK IS LOVE MADE VISIBLE.

Kahlil Gibran

DRAW THE WORK YOU LOVE:

The secret of joy in work is contained in one word—excellence. To know how to do something well is to enjoy it.

Pearl S. Buck

Work I excelled at today:

_____

_____

_____

DATE: _/_/_

FRIENDS WHO MULTIPLIED MY JOY TODAY:

_____

_____

_____

_____

_____

_____

_____

DATE: _/_/_

FRIENDS WHO DIVIDED MY GRIEFS TODAY:

_____

_____

_____

_____

_____

_____

_____

Friendships multiply joys and divide griefs.

Thomas Fuller

A joyful and pleasant thing it is to be thankful.

Bible, Psalm 147

What made me thankful today:

_____

_____

_____

Let us be grateful to people who make us happy; they are the charming gardeners who make our souls blossom.

Marcel Proust

Today's charming gardener:

_____

_____

_____

smile

AT A STRANGER

What happened?

_____

_____

_____

Joy is the feeling of grinning on the inside.

Melba Colgrove

What made me grin on the inside today:

_____

_____

_____

AN ACRE IN MIDDLESEX IS BETTER THAN A PRINCIPALITY IN UTOPIA.

Lord Macaulay

My better-than-Utopia:

_____

_____

_____

Eden is that old-fashioned House
We dwell in every day
Without suspecting our abode
Until we drive away.

Emily Dickinson

What makes my abode an Eden:

_____

_____

_____

IT WAS A DELIGHTFUL VISIT; —PERFECT, IN BEING MUCH TOO SHORT.

Jane Austen

DATE: __/__/__

TODAY I HAD A PERFECT VISIT TO:

_____

_____

_____

_____

_____

_____

_____

DATE: __/__/__

TODAY I HAD A PERFECT VISIT FROM:

_____

_____

_____

_____

_____

_____

_____

The man is richest whose pleasures are the cheapest.

Henry David Thoreau

My cheap pleasure today:

_____

_____

_____

HAPPINESS DEPENDS, AS NATURE SHOWS, LESS ON EXTERIOR THINGS THAN MOST SUPPOSE.

William Cowper

Something internal that brought happiness today:

_____

_____

_____

DATE: __/__/__

HAPPY FACE

DRAW YOUR FACE AFTER YOU HELPED SOMEONE TODAY.

The happiness of the tender heart is increased by what it can take away from the wretchedness of others.

Jean Antoine Petit-Senn

How my happiness increased by helping someone today:

_____

_____

_____

DATE: __/__/__

TOP
5

THE TOP FIVE FOODS THAT MAKE ME HAPPY

5 _____

4 _____

3 _____

2 _____

1 _____

Today I ate # _____

Talking of Pleasure . . .
a Nectarine—good God
how fine. It went down
soft, pulpy, slushy, oozy—
all its delicious embonpoint
melted down my throat like a
large beatified Strawberry.

John Keats

Describe the pleasure of eating something delicious today:

_____

_____

_____

DATE: __/__/__

HOW I COMMUNICATED MY PLEASURE TODAY:

_____

_____

_____

_____

_____

_____

_____

DATE: __/__/__

HOW I IMPARTED MY DELIGHT TODAY:

_____

_____

_____

_____

_____

_____

_____

No pleasure is fully delightsome without communication; and no delight absolute, except imparted.

Michel de Montaigne

If we could see the miracle of a single flower clearly, our whole life would change.

Buddha

The tiny miracle I saw in nature today:

_____

_____

_____

DATE: __/__/__

IF I HAD BUT TWO LOAVES OF BREAD, I WOULD SELL ONE OF THEM AND BUY WHITE HYACINTHS TO FEED MY SOUL.

Elbert Hubbard

My white hyacinths:

_____

_____

_____

I never did a day's work in my life. It was all fun.

Thomas Edison

Fun I had at work today:

_____

_____

_____

The supreme accomplishment is to blur the line between work and play.

Arnold Toynbee

Work I accomplished by playing today:

_____

_____

_____

DATE: __/__/__

WHAT WILL MAKE ME HAPPY NOW:

_____

_____

_____

_____

_____

_____

_____

DATE: __/__/__

WHAT WILL MAKE ME HAPPY HERE:

_____

_____

_____

_____

_____

_____

_____

THE TIME TO BE HAPPY IS NOW. THE PLACE TO BE HAPPY IS HERE.

Robert G. Ingersoll

Make us happy and you make us good!

Robert Browning

How I used my happiness for good today:

_____

_____

_____

I've learned that people will forget what you said, people will forget what you did, but people will never forget how you made them feel.

Maya Angelou

How someone made me feel happy:

_____

_____

_____

DATE: __/__/__

THE DELIGHTS OF MY DAY

Draw a balloon around
at least one.

A RAINBOW

THE SMELL
OF LILACS

A BUBBLE BATH

A KITTEN'S PURR

A PERSONAL
BEST

AN EMPTY
BEACH

FRESHLY
BREWED COFFEE

A STARRY
NIGHT

A JUICY PEACH

A CRACKLING FIRE

SOMETHING ELSE

_____

I am beginning to learn that it is the sweet, simple things of life that are the real ones after all.

Laura Ingalls Wilder

A sweet, simple thing that made me happy today:

_____

_____

_____

Danger and delight grow on one stalk.

English proverb

The danger in my delight today:

_____

_____

_____

Where there is no risk, there can be no pride in achievement and, consequently, no happiness.

Ray Kroc

The risk that made me proud—and happy—today:

_____

_____

_____

COUNT YOUR
BLESSINGS, NOT
YOUR CROSSES,
COUNT YOUR GAINS,
NOT YOUR LOSSES.

Proverb

DATE: __/__/__

TODAY'S BLESSINGS:

_____

_____

_____

_____

_____

_____

_____

DATE: __/__/__

TODAY'S GAINS:

_____

_____

_____

_____

_____

_____

_____

To be happy, drop the words "if only" and substitute instead the words "next time."

Smiley Blanton

~~If only~~

Next time _____

_____

_____

Never have to start sentences with "I should've…"

Peace Corps slogan

~~I should've~~

Today I _____

_____

_____

Laughter has always brought me out of unhappy situations. Even in your darkest moment, you usually can find something to laugh about if you try hard enough.

Red Skelton

What I laughed about in a dark moment today:

_____

_____

_____

LAUGH

IN THE DARK

How it felt:

_____

_____

_____

JUST BECAUSE YOU ARE HAPPY IT DOES NOT MEAN THAT THE DAY IS PERFECT BUT THAT YOU HAVE LOOKED BEYOND ITS IMPERFECTIONS.

Bob Marley

Imperfections I overlooked today:

_____

_____

_____

Happiness isn't good enough for me! I demand euphoria!

Bill Watterson

Today's euphoria:

_____

_____

_____

HAPPINESS LIES IN THE JOY OF ACHIEVEMENT AND THE THRILL OF CREATIVE EFFORT.

Franklin Delano Roosevelt

DATE: __/__/__

AN ACHIEVEMENT THAT GAVE ME JOY TODAY:

_____

_____

_____

_____

_____

_____

_____

DATE: __/__/__

A CREATIVE EFFORT THAT THRILLED ME TODAY:

_____

_____

_____

_____

_____

_____

_____

A man would have no pleasures in discovering all the beauties of the universe, even in heaven itself, unless he had a partner with whom he might share his joys.

Cicero

A partner with whom I share my joys:

_____

_____

_____

The clearest message that we get from this seventy-five-year study is this: Good relationships keep us happier and healthier.

Study of Adult Development, Harvard Medical School

The relationships that keep me happy and healthy:

_____

_____

_____

WHAT IS [MY] IDEA OF EARTHLY HAPPINESS? TO BE VINDICATED IN MY OWN LIFETIME.

Christopher Hitchens

How I was vindicated today:

_____

_____

_____

I'd far rather be happy than right any day.

Douglas Adams

Why I was happy, though wrong, today:

_____

_____

_____

DATE: __/__/__

TOP 5

THE TOP FIVE SONGS THAT MAKE ME HAPPY

5 _____

4 _____

3 _____

2 _____

1 _____

Today I listened to # _____

Words make you think a thought.
Music makes you feel a feeling.
A song makes you feel a thought.

E. Y. Harburg

Today the song _____

_____

made me feel this thought: _____

_____

_____

_____ .

DATE: __/__/__

TODAY I WAS HAPPY AND CAREFREE BECAUSE:

_____

_____

_____

_____

_____

_____

_____

DATE: __/__/__

TODAY I WAS CHEERFUL IN SPITE OF:

_____

_____

_____

_____

_____

_____

_____

A happy woman
is one who has
no cares at all;
a cheerful woman
is one who has
cares but
doesn't let them
get her down.

Beverly Sills

DATE: ___/___/___

It made me happy today to receive this gift:

_____

_____

_____

_____

from:

_____

_____

_____

DATE: _/_/_

It made me happy today to give this gift:

to:

The secret of happiness is not in doing what one likes, but in liking what one does.

J. M. Barrie

What I liked doing today:

_____

_____

_____

THE STRUGGLE THAT IS NOT JOYOUS IS THE WRONG STRUGGLE. THE JOY OF THE STRUGGLE IS NOT HEDONISM AND HILARITY, BUT THE SENSE OF PURPOSE, ACHIEVEMENT, AND DIGNITY.

Germaine Greer

My joyous struggle today:

_____

_____

_____

Anyone can be happy when times are good; the richer experience is to be happy when times are not.

Susan Harris

DATE: __/__/__

GOOD-TIME HAPPINESS TODAY:

_____

_____

_____

_____

_____

_____

_____

DATE: __/__/__

BAD-TIME HAPPINESS TODAY:

_____

_____

_____

_____

_____

_____

We act as though comfort and luxury were the chief requirements of life, when all that we need to make us really happy is something to be enthusiastic about.

Charles Kingsley

What I was enthusiastic about today:

_____

_____

_____

THE WORLD IS SO FULL
OF A NUMBER
OF THINGS,
I'M SURE WE SHOULD
ALL BE AS HAPPY
AS KINGS.

Robert Louis Stevenson

What made me as happy as a king today:

_____

_____

_____

Happiness in this world, when it comes, comes incidentally. Make it the object of pursuit, and it leads us a wild-goose chase, and is never attained.

Nathaniel Hawthorne

An incidental happiness today:

_____

_____

_____

NOW AND THEN IT'S GOOD TO PAUSE IN OUR PURSUIT OF HAPPINESS AND JUST BE HAPPY.

Guillaume Apollinaire

A happy pause today:

_____

_____

_____

DATE: __/__/__

WHERE I SOUGHT PLEASURE TODAY:

_____

_____

_____

_____

_____

_____

_____

DATE: __/__/__

HOW I AVOIDED PAIN TODAY:

_____

_____

_____

_____

_____

_____

_____

I seek
the utmost
pleasure
and the
least pain.

Plautus

If you have made another person on this earth smile, your life has been worthwhile.

Sr. Mary Christelle Macaluso

A person I made smile today:

_____

_____

_____

smile

AT SOMEONE IN UNIFORM

What happened?

_____

_____

_____

The less we indulge our pleasures, the more we enjoy them.

Juvenal

A rare pleasure enjoyed today:

_____

_____

_____

TO BE WITHOUT SOME OF THE THINGS YOU WANT IS AN INDISPENSABLE PART OF HAPPINESS.

Bertrand Russell

Some things I want that I'm without:

_____

_____

_____

DATE: __/__/__

Spring is nature's way of saying, "Let's party!"

Robin Williams

My spring party:

_____

_____

_____

Summer afternoon— summer afternoon... the two most beautiful words in the English language.

Henry James

My summer afternoon:

_____

_____

_____

DATE: _/_/_

HAPPY FACE

DRAW YOUR FACE WHILE YOU WERE BEING CREATIVE TODAY.

There is no greater joy than that of feeling oneself a creator. The triumph of life is expressed by creation.

Henri Bergson

What I created today:

_____

_____

_____

ALL MY LIFE THROUGH, THE NEW SIGHTS OF NATURE MADE ME REJOICE LIKE A CHILD.

Marie Curie

What new sights of nature made me rejoice today:

_____

_____

_____

DATE: __/__/__

TOP

5

THE TOP FIVE PLACES THAT MAKE ME HAPPY

5 _____

4 _____

3 _____

2 _____

1 _____

Today I visited # _____

DATE: __/__/__

HOW TRANQUILITY GAVE ME HAPPINESS TODAY:

_____

_____

_____

_____

_____

_____

_____

DATE: __/__/__

HOW OCCUPATION GAVE ME HAPPINESS TODAY:

_____

_____

_____

_____

_____

_____

_____

It is neither wealth nor splendor, but tranquility and occupation, that give happiness.

Thomas Jefferson

Happiness is neither virtue nor pleasure nor this thing nor that but simply growth. We are happy when we are growing.

William Butler Yeats

How I grew today:

_____

_____

_____

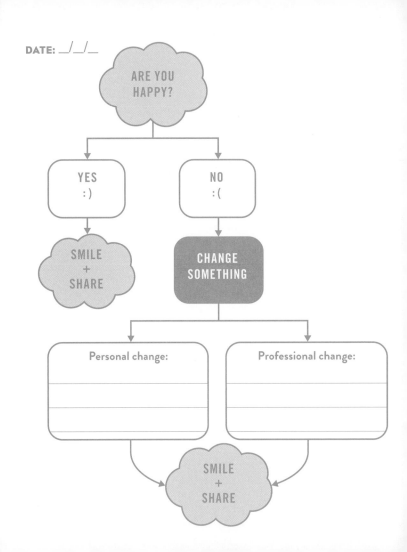

DATE: __/__/__

HAPPY HOLIDAY!

What made today a holiday:

Write it on your heart that every day is the best day of the year.

Ralph Waldo Emerson

Why today is the best day of the year:

_____

_____

_____

Sweets with joy delights in

DATE: __/__/__

AN EXTRA SWEETNESS TODAY:

sweets war not, joy.
▶ William Shakespeare

DATE: __/__/__

AN ADDED JOY TODAY:

Happiness is essentially a state of going somewhere, wholeheartedly, one-directionally, without regret or reservation.

William H. Sheldon

Today's destination:

_____

_____

_____

The really happy man is one who can enjoy the scenery on a detour.

Anonymous

The scenery on my detour today:

_____

_____

_____

DATE: __/__/__

THE DELIGHTS OF MY DAY

Draw a balloon around
at least one.

BREAKFAST
IN BED

A MASSAGE

A BIRD'S SONG

SKINNY-DIPPING

HOMEMADE
ICE CREAM

A SURPRISE
BOUQUET

A SMILE FROM
A STRANGER

A CLOUDLESS SKY

THE SMELL OF
AUTUMN LEAVES

COOKING
WITH FRIENDS

SOMETHING ELSE

_____

How simple and frugal a thing is happiness: a glass of wine, a roast chestnut, a wretched little brazier, the sound of the sea.

Nikos Kazantzakis

This simple, frugal thing brought me happiness today:

DATE: _/_/_

Cherish all your happy moments; they make a fine cushion for old age.

Christopher Morley

A happy moment I added to my cushion today:

_____

_____

_____

OLD AGE HAS ITS PLEASURES, WHICH, THOUGH DIFFERENT, ARE NOT LESS THAN THE PLEASURES OF YOUTH.

W. Somerset Maugham

The pleasures of my age now:

_____

_____

_____

DATE: __/__/__

MY PLEASURE IN THE WOODS TODAY:

_____

_____

_____

_____

_____

_____

_____

DATE: __/__/__

MY RAPTURE ON THE SHORE TODAY:

_____

_____

_____

_____

_____

_____

_____

THERE IS
A PLEASURE
IN THE
PATHLESS WOODS,
THERE IS A
RAPTURE ON THE
LONELY SHORE.

Lord Byron

Happiness hates the timid!

Eugene O'Neill

My courage today:

_____

_____

_____

THE SECRET OF REAPING THE GREATEST FRUITFULNESS AND THE GREATEST ENJOYMENT FROM LIFE IS TO LIVE DANGEROUSLY!

Friedrich Nietzsche

How I lived dangerously today:

_____

_____

_____

It has always seemed to me that hearty laughter is a good way to jog internally without having to go outdoors.

Norman Cousins

What made me jog internally today:

_____

_____

_____

LAUGH

IN THE MORNING

How it felt:

_____

_____

_____

A BLITHE HEART MAKES
A BLOOMING VISAGE.

Scottish proverb

MY BLOOMING VISAGE:

Happiness does away with ugliness, and even makes the beauty of beauty.

Henri-Frédéric Amiel

What my happiness beautified today:

_____

_____

_____

DATE: __/__/__

HOW I PUSHED MY BRAIN TODAY:

_____

_____

_____

_____

_____

_____

_____

DATE: __/__/__

HOW I PUSHED MY HEART TODAY:

_____

_____

_____

_____

_____

_____

_____

Happiness comes only when we push our brains and hearts to the farthest reaches of which we are capable.

Leo C. Rosten

Sanity and happiness are an impossible combination.

Mark Twain

What made me insanely happy today:

_____

_____

_____

I'm happy. Which often looks like crazy.

David Henry Hwang

What made me crazy happy today:

_____

_____

_____

Every job has drudgery.... The first secret of happiness is the recognition of this fundamental fact.

M. C. McIntosh

The drudgery I recognize in my job:

_____

_____

_____

THE TEST OF A VOCATION IS THE LOVE OF THE DRUDGERY IT INVOLVES.

Logan Pearsall Smith

The drudgery I love in my job:

_____

_____

_____

DATE: __/__/__

TOP

5

THE TOP FIVE PEOPLE WHO MAKE ME HAPPY

5 _____

4 _____

3 _____

2 _____

1 _____

Today I spent time with # _____

OF ALL THINGS THAT WISDOM PROVIDES TO MAKE US ENTIRELY HAPPY, MUCH THE GREATEST IS THE POSSESSION OF FRIENDSHIP.

Epicurus

This friendship made me happy today:

_____

_____

_____

DATE: __/__/__

A SONG I HEARD OR A POEM I READ TODAY:

_____

_____

_____

_____

_____

_____

_____

DATE: __/__/__

A PICTURE I SAW OR SENSIBLE WORDS I SPOKE TODAY:

_____

_____

_____

_____

_____

_____

_____

EVERY DAY WE SHOULD
HEAR AT LEAST
ONE LITTLE SONG,
READ ONE GOOD POEM,
SEE ONE EXQUISITE
PICTURE, AND,
IF POSSIBLE, SPEAK A
FEW SENSIBLE WORDS.

Johann Wolfgang von Goethe

DATE: __/__/__

It made me happy today to receive this compliment:

from:

DATE: _/_/_

It made me happy today to give this compliment

to:

Any man may
be in good spirits
and good temper
when he's
well dressed.

Charles Dickens

This outfit always puts me in good spirits:

_____

_____

_____

Where's the man could man could ease a heart Like a satin gown?

Dorothy Parker

This item of clothing eased my heart today:

_____

_____

_____

DATE: __/__/__

HOW CHEERFULNESS WAS FRIENDLY
TO MY MIND TODAY:

_____

_____

_____

_____

_____

_____

DATE: __/__/__

HOW CHEERFULNESS WAS FRIENDLY
TO MY BODY TODAY:

_____

_____

_____

_____

_____

_____

Cheerfulness is the best promoter of health and is as friendly to the mind as to the body.

Joseph Addison

The butterfly counts not months but moments, and has time enough.

Rabindranath Tagore

Today I enjoyed these moments:

_____

_____

_____

Don't cry because it's over. Smile because it happened.

Dr. Seuss

I smiled because this happened today:

_____

_____

_____

You have to be willing to get happy about nothing.

Andy Warhol

Why I was happy about nothing today:

_____

_____

_____

There's no greater bliss in life than when the plumber eventually comes to unblock your drains.

Victoria Glendinning

Today's humble bliss:

_____

_____

_____

All animals, except man, know that the principal business of life is to enjoy it.

Samuel Butler

How I enjoyed life today:

_____

_____

_____

DATE: __/__/__

HAPPINESS TO A DOG IS WHAT LIES ON THE OTHER SIDE OF THE DOOR.

Charlton Ogburn, Jr.

What lies on the other side of my door today:

_____

_____

_____

DATE: __/__/__

BUSINESS THAT WAS A PLEASURE TODAY:

_____

_____

_____

_____

_____

_____

_____

DATE: __/__/__

PLEASURE THAT WAS MY BUSINESS TODAY:

_____

_____

_____

_____

_____

_____

_____

The rule of my life is to make business a pleasure, and pleasure my business.

Aaron Burr

DRAW YOUR PLEASURE, PAINT YOUR PLEASURE, AND EXPRESS YOUR PLEASURE STRONGLY.

Pierre Bonnard

DRAW, PAINT, EXPRESS:

The soul's joy lies in doing.

Percy Bysshe Shelley

Doing this brought me joy today:

_____

_____

_____

It was only a sunny smile,
and little it cost in the
giving, but like morning
light it scattered the
night and made the day
worth living.

F. Scott Fitzgerald

A sunny smile that made this day worth living:

smile

IN A STORE OR RESTAURANT

What happened?

_____

_____

_____

THE SUNSHINE OF LIFE IS MADE UP OF VERY LITTLE BEAMS THAT ARE BRIGHT ALL THE TIME.

John Aikin

My bright little beams:

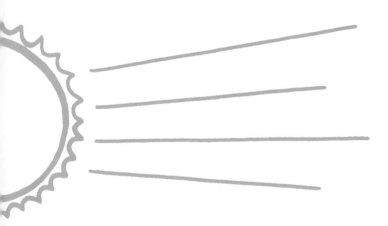

Happiness is a sunbeam that may pass through a thousand bosoms without losing a particle of its original ray.

Sir Philip Sidney

My undiluted happiness passed through these people:

_____, _____,

_____, _____,

_____, and _____.

DATE: ___/___/___

WHAT MADE ME LAUGH TODAY:

_____

_____

_____

_____

_____

_____

_____

DATE: ___/___/___

HOW I MADE THE WORLD LAUGH TODAY:

_____

_____

_____

_____

_____

_____

_____

Laugh, and the world laughs with you; Weep, and you weep alone.

Ella Wheeler Wilcox

I love to sail forbidden seas, and land on barbarous coasts.

Herman Melville

Dangers I loved today:

_____

_____

_____

Who is the happier man, he who has braved the storm of life and lived or he who has stayed securely on shore and merely existed?

Hunter S. Thompson

A storm I braved today:

_____

_____

_____

DATE: __/__/__

HAPPY FACE

DRAW YOUR FACE WHEN YOU WERE ACTIVE TODAY.

HAPPINESS IS ACTION.

David Thomas

This action brought me happiness today:

_____

_____

_____

DATE: __/__/__

When someone does something well, applaud! You will make two people happy.

Samuel Goldwyn

How applauding _____ today

made us both happy: _____

_____

_____

TOP 5

THE TOP FIVE SHOWS THAT MAKE ME HAPPY

5 _____

4 _____

3 _____

2 _____

1 _____

Today I watched or saw # _____

DATE: __/__/__

SOMETHING SOFT AND LIGHT
THAT MADE THE BEST HAPPINESS TODAY:

_____

_____

_____

_____

_____

_____

DATE: __/__/__

A MOMENT'S GLANCE
THAT MADE THE BEST HAPPINESS TODAY:

_____

_____

_____

_____

_____

_____

PRECISELY THE LEAST,
THE SOFTEST,
LIGHTEST, A LIZARD'S
RUSTLING, A BREATH,
A BREEZE, A MOMENT'S
GLANCE—IT IS <u>LITTLE</u>
THAT MAKES
THE <u>BEST</u> HAPPINESS.

Friedrich Nietzsche

DATE: __/__/__

HAPPY HOLIDAY!

What made my birthday happy:

DATE: __/__/__

We turn not older with years, but newer every day.

Emily Dickinson

How I turned newer today:

_____

_____

_____

DATE: __/__/__

WHEN IN DOUBT, WEAR RED.

Bill Blass

Something red that made me happy today:

_____

_____

_____

Green, how I love you, green. Green wind. Green branches.

Federico García Lorca

Something green that made me happy today:

_____

_____

_____

There are two things to aim at in life: first, to get what you want, and after that to enjoy it. Only the wisest of mankind achieve the second.

Logan Pearsall Smith

DATE: __/__/__

WHAT I GOT THAT I WANTED TODAY:

_____

_____

_____

_____

_____

_____

_____

DATE: __/__/__

HOW I ENJOYED WHAT I GOT TODAY:

_____

_____

_____

_____

_____

_____

_____

THE HAPPIEST OF ALL LIVES IS A BUSY SOLITUDE.

Voltaire

How my busy solitude made me happy today:

_____

_____

_____

I liked to sail alone. The sea was the same as a girl to me— I did not want anyone else along.

E. B. White

What I liked doing alone today:

_____

_____

_____

DATE: __/__/__

THE DELIGHTS OF MY DAY

Draw a balloon around
at least one.

A COMPLIMENT

A PUPPY'S
NUZZLE

THE SOUND
OF WAVES

RAINDROPS ON THE ROOF

A SUNRISE

FOUND MONEY

A SNOW DAY

A HOT TOWEL

A CHILD'S SNUGGLE

THE FIRST
MORNING STRETCH

SOMETHING ELSE

_____

DATE: __/__/__

One of the secrets of a happy life is continuous small treats.

Iris Murdoch

Today's small treat:

_____

_____

_____

The best thing for being sad . . . is to learn something.

T. H. White

What I learned today:

_____

_____

_____

Pleasures of the mind have this advantage— they never cloy nor wear themselves out, but increase by employment.

Frances Power Cobbe

A pleasure of the mind I employed today:

_____

_____

_____

The one thing we can never
And the one thing we never

DATE: __/__/__

LOVE I GOT TODAY:

get enough of is love.
give enough of is love. ▶ *Henry Miller*

DATE: __/__/__

LOVE I GAVE TODAY:

The secret of life is to have a task, something you devote your entire life to, something you bring everything to, every minute of the day for your whole life. And the most important thing is— it must be something you cannot possibly do!

Henry Moore

My impossible task:

_____

What I brought to it today:

_____

Satisfaction lies in the effort, not in the attainment. Full effort is full victory.

Mohandas Karamchand Gandhi

My full effort today:

_____

_____

_____

DATE: __/__/__

LAUGHTER IS THE SUN WHICH DRIVES WINTER FROM THE HUMAN FACE.

Victor Hugo

The laughter that drove off winter today:

_____

_____

_____

LAUGH

AT WORK

How it felt:

_____

_____

_____

Those who are happiest are those who do the most for others.

Booker T. Washington

What I did for another today:

_____

_____

_____

I SHALL TAKE THE HEART...
FOR BRAINS DO NOT MAKE
ONE HAPPY, AND HAPPINESS
IS THE BEST THING IN
THE WORLD.

L. Frank Baum

How using my heart made me happy today:

_____

_____

_____

FOR THE GOOD ARE
ALWAYS THE MERRY,
SAVE BY AN
EVIL CHANCE,
AND THE MERRY LOVE
THE FIDDLE,
AND THE MERRY
LOVE TO DANCE.

William Butler Yeats

DATE: __/__/__

HOW I FIDDLED MERRILY TODAY:

_____

_____

_____

_____

_____

_____

_____

DATE: __/__/__

HOW I DANCED MERRILY TODAY:

_____

_____

_____

_____

_____

_____

_____

ONE HOUR OF JOY DISPELS THE CARES AND SUFFERINGS OF A THOUSAND YEARS.

Nicolas Anselme Baptiste

My hour of joy today:

_____

_____

_____

The way I see it, if you want the rainbow, you gotta put up with the rain.

Dolly Parton

Today's rain:

_____

Today's rainbow:

_____

_____

I wish I could freeze this moment, right here, right now, and live in it forever.

Suzanne Collins

A moment I would like to live in forever:

_____

_____

_____

My advice to you
is not to inquire
why or whither,
but just enjoy your
ice cream while
it's on your plate.

Thornton Wilder

Today's ice cream:

_____

_____

_____

DATE: __/__/__

TOP 5

THE TOP FIVE ANIMALS THAT MAKE ME HAPPY

5 _____

4 _____

3 _____

2 _____

1 _____

Today I played with # _____

I don't know how happiness could get any more perfect, but I think it would involve more puppies.

Ellen DeGeneres

My perfect happiness would involve more

_____

_____

_____

DATE: __/__/__

TODAY'S NOBLE DEED:

_____

_____

_____

_____

_____

_____

_____

DATE: __/__/__

TODAY'S HOT BATH:

_____

_____

_____

_____

_____

_____

_____

NOBLE DEEDS AND HOT BATHS ARE THE BEST CURES FOR DEPRESSION.

Dodie Smith

It made me happy today to get a hug from

because

It made me happy today to give a hug to

because

To business that we love we rise betime, And go to't with delight.

William Shakespeare

What I rose with delight to do today:

_____

_____

_____

OH, GIVE US THE MAN WHO SINGS AT HIS WORK.

Thomas Carlyle

Why I sang at work today:

_____

_____

_____

None are happy, but by the anticipation of change.

Samuel Johnson

What I look forward to changing today:

_____

_____

_____

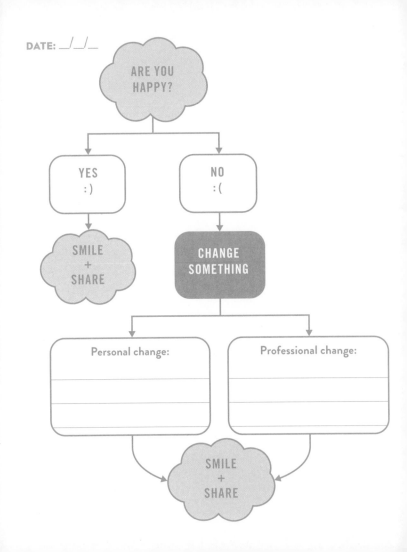

HAPPINESS IS REFLECTIVE, LIKE THE LIGHT OF HEAVEN.

Washington Irving

DATE: __/__/__

MY HAPPINESS TODAY:

_____

_____

_____

IT REFLECTED FROM:

_____

_____

_____

DATE: __/__/__

MY HAPPINESS TODAY:

_____

_____

_____

IT REFLECTED ONTO:

_____

_____

_____

There is a road from the eye to the heart that does not go through the intellect.

G. K. Chesterton

A sight that went right to my heart today:

_____

_____

_____

A thing of beauty is a joy forever.

John Keats

A thing of beauty I

[ ] saw: _____

[ ] held: _____

[ ] created: _____

[ ] remembered: _____

_____

THE TEST OF PLEASURE IS THE MEMORY IT LEAVES BEHIND.

Jean Paul Richter

A memory that brought me pleasure today:

_____

_____

_____

DATE: __/__/__

All the great pleasures in life are silent.

Georges Clemenceau

Today's silent pleasure:

_____

_____

_____

Remember that happiness is as contagious as gloom. It should be the first duty of those who are happy to let others know of their gladness.

Maurice Maeterlinck

I infected these people with my gladness today:

_____

_____

_____

All who joy would win Must share it – Happiness was born a twin.

Lord Byron

Today I shared my joy with _____

_____

_____

_____

DATE: __/__/__

PLEASURES THAT RECREATE MUCH:

_____

_____

_____

_____

_____

_____

DATE: __/__/__

PLEASURES THAT COST LITTLE:

_____

_____

_____

_____

_____

_____

CHOOSE SUCH PLEASURES AS RECREATE MUCH, AND COST LITTLE.

Richard Fuller

A GOOD ROUSING SNEEZE, ONE THAT TEARS OPEN YOUR COLLAR AND THROWS YOUR HAIR INTO YOUR EYES, IS REALLY ONE OF LIFE'S SENSATIONAL PLEASURES.

Robert Benchley

My sensational sneeze today:

_____

_____

_____

Scratching is one of nature's sweetest gratifications, and the one nearest at hand.

Michel de Montaigne

Where scratching felt sweetest today:

_____

_____

_____

smile

IN THE MIRROR

What happened?

_____

_____

_____

A smile is the best makeup any girl can wear.

Marilyn Monroe

Where I wore my smile today:

_____

_____

_____

Hard is his herte that loveth nought In May, whan al this mirth is wrought.

Geoffrey Chaucer

My love this day in May:

_____

_____

_____

What is so rare as a day in June? Then, if ever, come perfect days.

James Russell Lowell

My perfect June day:

_____

_____

_____

The highlights
of my life have been
innumerable. . . .
But I think
the real highlight
is the persistent
feeling that the best
is yet to come.

Mort Schindel

DATE: __/__/__

THE HIGHLIGHTS OF MY LIFE:

_____

_____

_____

_____

_____

_____

_____

DATE: __/__/__

WHAT I HOPE IS YET TO COME:

_____

_____

_____

_____

_____

_____

_____

DATE: __/__/__

WHEN ONE HAS TASTED [WATERMELON], HE KNOWS WHAT THE ANGELS EAT.

Mark Twain

Today's watermelon:

_____

_____

_____

DATE: __/__/__

THE TASTE OF CHOCOLATE IS A SENSUAL PLEASURE IN ITSELF, EXISTING IN THE SAME WORLD AS SEX.

Dr. Ruth Westheimer

What I tasted today that gave me a sensual pleasure:

_____

_____

_____

HAPPY FACE

DRAW YOUR FACE WHEN YOU FELT GRATEFUL TODAY.

DATE: __/__/__

In every exalted joy, there mingles a sense of gratitude.

Marie von Ebner-Eschenbach

Today's exalted joy:

_____

_____

This made me grateful for:

_____

_____

DATE: __/__/__

TOP

5

THE TOP FIVE BOOKS THAT MAKE ME HAPPY

5 _____

4 _____

3 _____

2 _____

1 _____

Today I read # _____

Poetry is the record of the best and happiest moments of the happiest and best minds.

Percy Bysshe Shelley

This poem made me happy today:

_____

_____

_____

DATE: __/__/__

HOW MY MIND WAS SOUND TODAY:

_____

_____

_____

_____

_____

_____

_____

DATE: __/__/__

HOW MY BODY WAS SOUND TODAY:

_____

_____

_____

_____

_____

_____

_____

A SOUND MIND IN A SOUND BODY IS A SHORT BUT FULL DESCRIPTION OF A HAPPY STATE IN THIS WORLD.

John Locke

DATE: __/__/__

HAPPY HOLIDAY!

What made this holiday with my family happy:

_____

_____

_____

Hurrah for the fun!
Is the pudding done?
Hurrah for the
pumpkin pie!

Lydia Maria Child

Holiday foods that make me happy:

_____

_____

_____

The greatest pleasure in life is doing what people say you cannot do.

Walter Bagehot

What gave me great pleasure to do against the odds today:

_____

_____

_____

"And hast thou slain the
   Jabberwock?
Come to my arms,
   my beamish boy!
O frabjous day! Callooh!
   Callay!"
He chortled in his joy.

Lewis Carroll

A Jabberwock I slew today:

_____

_____

_____

I look out the window and I see the lights and the skyline and the people on the street rushing around looking for action, love, and the world's greatest chocolate chip cookie, and my heart does a little dance.

Nora Ephron

My heart does a little dance when I see _____

_____

_____

_____.

DATE: __/__/__

TODAY ME WILL LIVE IN THE MOMENT UNLESS IT'S UNPLEASANT IN WHICH CASE ME WILL EAT A COOKIE.

Cookie Monster

A cookie that made today pleasant:

_____

_____

_____

OH HOW THRICE AND FOUR TIMES HAPPY ARE THOSE WHO PLANT CABBAGES!

François Rabelais

How a garden made me happy today:

_____

_____

_____

And since to look
    at things in bloom
Fifty springs are little room,
About the woodlands
    I will go
To see the cherry
    hung with snow.

A. E. Housman

A happy woodlands walk today:

_____

_____

_____

DATE: __/__/__

THE DELIGHTS OF MY DAY

Draw a balloon around
at least one.

SILENCE

A WALK IN
THE PARK

WARM, SOFT
CHOCOLATE
CHIP COOKIES

A COMPLETED
PUZZLE

SAND IN
MY TOES

THE MORNING DEW

SNOW ON TREE
BRANCHES

A SHARED JOKE

A HAPPY SURPRISE

SOMETHING ELSE

THE SMELL
OF PEPPERMINT

_____

A multitude of small delights constitute happiness.

Charles Baudelaire

Today's small delights:

_____

_____

_____

The world is good-natured to people who are good-natured.

William Makepeace Thackeray

How the world reflected my good nature today:

_____

_____

_____

DATE: __/__/__

The greater part of
our happiness or
misery depends upon
our dispositions,
and not upon our
circumstances.

Martha Washington

How my disposition affected my happiness today:

_____

_____

_____

DATE: __/__/__

HOW MY FRIEND'S JOY REBOUNDED UPON ME TODAY:

_____

_____

_____

_____

_____

_____

DATE: __/__/__

HOW MY FRIEND'S BRIGHT CANDLE LIT MINE TODAY:

_____

_____

_____

_____

_____

_____

The very Society of Joy redoubl[es] it:
so that while it lights directly upon my Friend,
it rebounds upon myself;
and the brighter his Candle burns, the more easily will it light mine.

Robert South

Happiness is like a butterfly that appears and delights us for one brief moment, but soon flits away.

Anna Pavlova

My brief moment of happiness today:

_____

_____

_____

DATE: __/__/__

Happiness makes up in height for what it lacks in length.

Robert Frost

My happiness today:

_____

_____

Its height (1–10):

_____

Its length (1–10):

_____

LAUGHING DEEPLY IS LIVING DEEPLY.

Milan Kundera

How I lived deeply today:

_____

_____

_____

LAUGH

OUTDOORS

How it felt:

_____

_____

_____

I love everything that's old: old friends, old times, old manners, old books, old wine.

Oliver Goldsmith

Old things I love:

_____

_____

_____

Nothing is so perfectly amusement as a total change of ideas.

Laurence Sterne

Today's new idea:

_____

_____

_____

It is the mynd
that maketh
good or ill,
that maketh
wretch or happie,
rich or poore.

Edmund Spenser

DATE: __/__/__

HOW MY MIND MADE ME FEEL GOOD, NOT ILL, TODAY:

_____

_____

_____

DATE: __/__/__

HOW MY MIND MADE ME FEEL HAPPY, NOT WRETCHED, TODAY:

_____

_____

_____

DATE: __/__/__

HOW MY MIND MADE ME FEEL RICH, NOT POOR, TODAY:

_____

_____

_____

PEOPLE FROM A PLANET WITHOUT FLOWERS WOULD THINK WE MUST BE MAD WITH JOY THE WHOLE TIME TO HAVE SUCH THINGS ABOUT US.

Iris Murdoch

Flowers that make me mad with joy:

_____

_____

_____

My heart leaps up when I behold A rainbow in the sky.

William Wordsworth

How a rainbow made me feel:

_____

_____

_____

True love always ourself, and to the

DATE: __/__/__

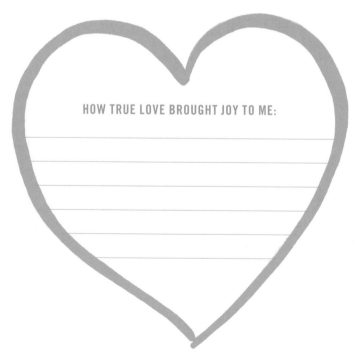

HOW TRUE LOVE BROUGHT JOY TO ME:

brings joy to one we love. ▶ *Thich Nhat Hanh*

DATE: _/_/_

HOW TRUE LOVE BROUGHT JOY TO THE ONE I LOVE:

Some people never find it
Some, only pretend,
  but me:
I just want to live
  happily ever after
  every now and then.

Jimmy Buffett

How I lived happily ever after today:

_____

_____

_____

They say it is better to be poor and happy than rich and miserable, but how about a compromise like moderately rich and just moody?

Diana, Princess of Wales

My happiness compromise today:

_____

_____

_____

What I dream of is an art of balance, of purity and serenity devoid of troubling or depressing subject matter.

Henri Matisse

The art I dream of:

_____

_____

_____

TOP

5

**THE TOP FIVE WORKS OF ART
THAT MAKE ME HAPPY**

5 _____

4 _____

3 _____

2 _____

1 _____

Today I looked at # _____

DATE: __/__/__

THE SUPERFLUITIES I DO NOT REQUIRE TODAY:

_____

_____

_____

_____

_____

_____

DATE: __/__/__

THE NECESSARIES I HAVE TODAY:

_____

_____

_____

_____

_____

_____

That state of life
is most happy
where superfluities
are not required
and necessaries are
not wanting.

Plutarch

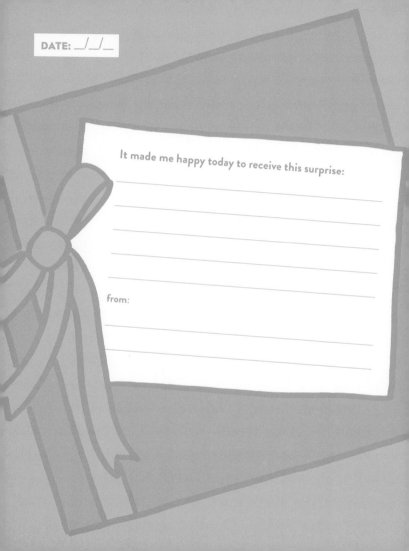

DATE: __/__/__

It made me happy today to receive this surprise:

from:

It made me happy today to give this surprise:

to:

Don't wait around for other people to be happy for you. Any happiness you get you've got to make yourself.

Alice Walker

Happiness I made for myself today:

_____

_____

_____

When a man is gloomy, everything seems to go wrong; when he is cheerful, everything seems right!

Bible, Proverbs 15:15

What today's cheer made right:

_____

_____

_____

DATE: ___/___/___

THE HAPPINESS THAT DEPENDED ON MY COURAGE TODAY:

_____

_____

_____

_____

_____

_____

_____

DATE: ___/___/___

THE HAPPINESS THAT DEPENDED ON MY WORK TODAY:

_____

_____

_____

_____

_____

_____

All happiness
depends on
courage
and work.

Honoré de Balzac

ALL YOU NEED IS LOVE.

John Lennon and Paul McCartney

How love brought me happiness today:

_____

_____

_____

If love is the best thing in life, then the best part of love is the kiss.

Thomas Mann

The kiss I loved today:

_____

_____

_____

DATE: __/__/__

ENERGY IS ETERNAL DELIGHT.

William Blake

What made me energetic today:

_____

_____

_____

Oh, the wild joys of living!

Robert Browning

Today's wild joy:

_____

_____

_____

To love what you do how could anything else

WHY I LOVE WHAT I DO:

and feel that it matters— be more fun? ▶ *Katharine Graham*

DATE: __/__/__

WHY WHAT I DO MATTERS:

A mind always employed is always happy. This is the true secret, the grand recipe for felicity.

Thomas Jefferson

How I employed my mind today:

_____

_____

_____

DATE: __/__/__

Knowledge is ecstatic in enjoyment, perennial in fame, unlimited in space, and infinite in duration.

De Witt Clinton

Knowledge that made me ecstatic today:

_____

_____

_____

I frequently tramped eight or ten miles through the deepest snow to keep an appointment with a beech tree, or a yellow-birch, or an old acquaintance among the pines.

Henry David Thoreau

Natural beauty I tramped far to reach today:

_____

_____

_____

My mountain did not seem
to me a lifeless thing
of rock and ice, but warm
and friendly and living.
She was a mother hen, and
the other mountains were
chicks under her wings.

Tenzing Norgay

My warm and friendly and living mountain today:

_____

_____

_____

WRINKLES SHOULD MERELY INDICATE WHERE SMILES HAVE BEEN.

Mark Twain

The smiles that made my wrinkles:

_____

_____

_____

DATE: __/__/__

smile

AS SOON AS YOU WAKE UP

What happened?

_____

_____

_____

Family life is the source of the greatest human happiness.

Robert J. Havighurst

How my family made me happy today:

_____

_____

_____

WHEN THE VOICES OF CHILDREN
  ARE HEARD ON THE GREEN,
AND LAUGHING IS HEARD ON THE HILL,
MY HEART IS AT REST
  WITHIN MY BREAST,
AND EVERYTHING ELSE IS STILL.

William Blake

How children brought me happiness today:

_____

_____

_____

DATE: __/__/__

HOW I BECAME HAPPY TODAY:

_____

_____

_____

_____

_____

_____

_____

DATE: __/__/__

MY TALENT FOR HAPPINESS:

_____

_____

_____

_____

_____

_____

_____

Happiness
is a how,
not a what;
a talent, not
an object.

Hermann Hesse

Joy is the best of wine.

George Eliot

My intoxicating joy today:

_____

_____

_____

With true friends ...even water drunk together is sweet.

Chinese proverb

Today's sweet, simple meal with friends:

_____

_____

_____

DATE: __/__/__

HAPPY FACE

DRAW YOUR FACE WHILE YOU WERE HAPPY
DOING NOTHING TODAY.

The time you enjoy wasting is not wasted time.

Bertrand Russell

How I enjoyed wasting time today:

_____

_____

_____

DATE: ___/___/___

TOP

5

THE TOP FIVE OUTDOOR ACTIVITIES
THAT MAKE ME HAPPY

5 _____

4 _____

3 _____

2 _____

1 _____

Today I did # _____

DATE: __/__/__

NOTHING COMPARES TO THE SIMPLE PLEASURE OF A BIKE RIDE.

John F. Kennedy

Today's bike ride:

_____

_____

_____

DATE: __/__/__

THE DEEDS I DID WELL TODAY:

_____

_____

_____

_____

_____

_____

_____

DATE: __/__/__

THE NEW THINGS I CREATED TODAY:

_____

_____

_____

_____

_____

_____

_____

TRUE HAPPINESS
COMES FROM
THE JOY OF DEEDS
WELL DONE,
THE ZEST
OF CREATING
THINGS NEW.

Antoine de Saint-Exupéry

One half of the world cannot understand the pleasures of the other.

Jane Austen

A pleasure of mine that no one can understand:

_____

_____

_____

DATE: __/__/__

A private holiday I celebrate:

_____

_____

_____

My candle burns at
  both ends;
It will not last
  the night;
But ah, my foes, and
  oh, my friends—
It gives a lovely light!

Edna St. Vincent Millay

My night of lovely light:

_____

_____

_____

Life is no "brief candle"
for me. It is a sort of splendid
torch, which I have got hold
of for the moment; and I want
to make it burn as brightly
as possible before handing it
on to future generations.

George Bernard Shaw

My splendid torch:

_____

_____

_____

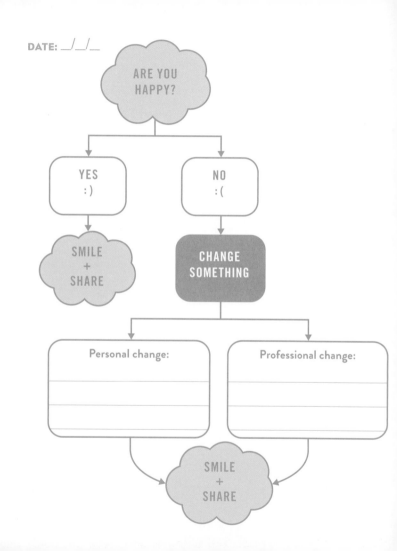

DATE: __/__/__

A merry heart doeth good like a medicine.

Bible, Proverbs 17:22

How a merry heart healed me today:

_____

_____

_____

DATE: __/__/__

MY LITTLE DEED OF KINDNESS TODAY:

_____

_____

_____

_____

_____

_____

_____

DATE: __/__/__

MY LITTLE WORD OF LOVE TODAY:

_____

_____

_____

_____

_____

_____

_____

Little deeds
of kindness,
Little words
of love,
Help to make
earth happy,
Like the
heaven above.

Julia A. Fletcher Carney

ACTION MAY NOT ALWAYS BRING HAPPINESS; BUT THERE IS NO HAPPINESS WITHOUT ACTION.

Benjamin Disraeli

An action that made me happy today:

_____

_____

_____

One hour of life,
crowded to the full
with glorious action, and
filled with noble risks,
is worth whole years of
those mean observances
of paltry decorum.

Sir Walter Scott

My one hour of action and risk today:

_____

_____

_____

DATE: __/__/__

THE DELIGHTS OF MY DAY

Draw a balloon around
at least one.

PLAYING
HOOKY

A SLEEPING
BABY

POWDERY SNOW

A FOUR-LEAF
CLOVER

AN ICE-COLD
DRINK

A COMPLETED
TO-DO LIST

BIKING WITH
A FRIEND

A HAPPY CHILDHOOD
MEMORY

CHOCOLATE-COVERED
STRAWBERRIES

A HANDMADE GIFT

SOMETHING ELSE

_____

DATE: __/__/__

ENJOY THE LITTLE THINGS IN LIFE, FOR ONE DAY YOU MAY LOOK BACK AND REALIZE THEY WERE THE BIG THINGS.

Robert Brault

A little thing I enjoyed that turned out to be a big thing:

_____

_____

_____

The formula for complete happiness is to be very busy with the unimportant.

A. Edward Newton

The unimportant thing that kept me busy today:

_____

_____

_____

Each day provides its own gifts.

Martial

Today's gifts:

_____

_____

_____

True happiness . . .
arises, in the first place,
from the enjoyment
of one's self; and
in the next, from
the friendship and
conversation of a few
select companions.

Joseph Addison

DATE: __/__/__

ENJOYMENT OF MYSELF TODAY:

_____

_____

_____

_____

_____

_____

_____

DATE: __/__/__

ENJOYMENT OF FRIENDSHIP AND CONVERSATION TODAY:

_____

_____

_____

_____

_____

_____

IF YOU RESOLVE TO GIVE UP SMOKING, DRINKING, AND LOVING, YOU DON'T ACTUALLY LIVE LONGER; IT JUST SEEMS LONGER.

Clement Freud

My life would seem longer without:

_____

_____

_____

All the things I really like to do are either immoral, illegal, or fattening.

Alexander Woollcott

My guiltiest pleasure:

_____

_____

_____

LAUGH

IN THE SHOWER

How it felt:

_____

_____

_____

A good laugh is sunshine in a house.

William Makepeace Thackeray

How I lit up the house today:

_____

_____

_____

I finally figured out the only reason to be alive is to enjoy it.

Rita Mae Brown

How I enjoyed being alive today:

_____

_____

_____

DATE: __/__/__

HAPPINESS IS A SMALL AND UNWORTHY GOAL FOR SOMETHING AS BIG AND FANCY AS A WHOLE LIFETIME, AND SHOULD BE TAKEN IN SMALL DOSES.

Russell Baker

My small dose of happiness today:

_____

_____

_____

Pleasure is very seldom found where it is sought. Our brightest blazes of gladness are commonly kindled by unexpected sparks.

Samuel Johnson

An unexpected spark of pleasure today:

_____

_____

_____

I have always been delighted at the prospect of a new day, a fresh try, one more start, with perhaps a bit of magic waiting somewhere behind the morning.

J. B. Priestley

The bit of magic behind this morning:

_____

_____

_____

Happiness is not an ideal of reason but of imagination.

Immanuel Kant

The happiness I imagined today:

_____

_____

_____

DATE: __/__/__

TOP

5

THE TOP FIVE CREATIVE ACTIVITIES
THAT MAKE ME HAPPY

5 _____

4 _____

3 _____

2 _____

1 _____

Today I did # _____

DATE: ___/___/___

HOW I SOUGHT TO SERVE TODAY:

_____

_____

_____

_____

_____

_____

_____

DATE: ___/___/___

HOW I FOUND TO SERVE TODAY:

_____

_____

_____

_____

_____

_____

_____

The only ones among you who will be really happy are those who will have sought and found how to serve.

Albert Schweitzer

DATE: __/__/__

It made me happy today to receive this text:

_____

_____

_____

_____

_____

from:

_____

_____

It made me happy today to send this text:

to:

THE GREAT SECRET OF HUMAN HAPPINESS IS THIS: NEVER SUFFER YOUR ENERGIES TO STAGNATE. THE OLD ADAGE OF "TOO MANY IRONS IN THE FIRE" CONVEYS AN ABOMINABLE LIE.

Adam Clarke

My irons in the fire:

_____

_____

_____

You're happiest while you're making the greatest contribution.

Robert F. Kennedy

My great contribution today:

_____

_____

_____

DATE: __/__/__

MY HEALTH TODAY:

_____

_____

_____

DATE: __/__/__

MY PEACE TODAY:

_____

_____

_____

DATE: __/__/__

MY COMPETENCE TODAY:

_____

_____

_____

REASON'S WHOLE
PLEASURE,
ALL THE JOYS
OF SENSE,
LIE IN THREE WORDS,
HEALTH, PEACE,
AND COMPETENCE.

Alexander Pope

NO ONE IN THIS WORLD NEEDS A MINK COAT BUT A MINK.

Anonymous

A luxury I don't need in order to be happy:

_____

_____

_____

The superfluous is very necessary.

Voltaire

Something superfluous I need to be happy:

_____

_____

_____

To live long and achieve happiness, cultivate the art of radiating happiness.

Malcolm Forbes

How I radiated happiness today:

_____

_____

_____

Make one person
happy each day, and
in forty years you
will have made 14,600
human beings happy
for a little time at least.

Charley Willey

Today I made _____ happy by

_____

_____

_____

It's good to play, and you must keep in practice.

Jerry Seinfeld

How I practiced playing today:

HAPPINESS IS A THING TO BE PRACTICED, LIKE THE VIOLIN.

Sir John Lubbock

How I practiced happiness today:

_____

_____

_____

Pleasure is
necessarily reciprocal;
no one feels [it],
who does not
at the same time
give it.
To be pleased,
one must please.

Lord Chesterfield

DATE: __/__/__

PLEASURE I GAVE TODAY:

_____

_____

_____

_____

_____

_____

_____

DATE: __/__/__

PLEASURE I FELT TODAY:

_____

_____

_____

_____

_____

_____

_____

To find out what
one is fitted to do
and to secure an
opportunity to do it is
the key to happiness.

John Dewey

What I am fitted to do:

_____

_____

My opportunity to do it:

_____

_____

Find something you're passionate about and keep tremendously interested in it.

Julia Child

My passion:

_____

_____

_____

Sometimes your joy is the source of your smile, but sometimes your smile can be the source of your joy.

Thich Nhat Hanh

How my smile was the source of my joy today:

_____

_____

_____

smile

AT A SERVER, ATTENDANT, OR RECEPTIONIST

What happened?

_____

_____

_____

MAKE HAPPY THOSE WHO ARE NEAR, AND THOSE WHO ARE FAR WILL COME.

Chinese proverb

People nearby I made happy today:

_____

_____

Others who came to join us:

_____

_____

The foolish man seeks happiness in the distance; The wise grows it under his feet.

James Oppenheim

Happiness I grew under my feet today:

_____

_____

_____

DATE: __/__/__

HOW I LIVED IN THE SUNSHINE TODAY:

_____

_____

_____

DATE: __/__/__

HOW I SWAM THE SEA TODAY:

_____

_____

_____

DATE: __/__/__

HOW I DRANK THE WILD AIR TODAY:

_____

_____

_____

LIVE IN THE SUNSHINE, SWIM THE SEA, DRINK THE WILD AIR'S SALUBRITY.

Ralph Waldo Emerson

To joys too exquisite to last, —And yet *more* exquisite when past!

James Montgomery

The memory of an exquisite joy:

_____

_____

_____

Mankind are always happier for having been happy; so that if you make them happy now, you make them happy twenty years hence by memory of it.

Sydney Smith

A happy memory I made today:

_____

_____

_____

DATE: __/__/__

HAPPY FACE

DRAW YOUR FACE WHEN YOU FELT HOPEFUL TODAY.

DATE: __/__/__

Hope is itself a species of happiness, and, perhaps, the chief happiness that this world affords.

Samuel Johnson

My happy hope today:

_____

_____

_____

DATE: __/__/__

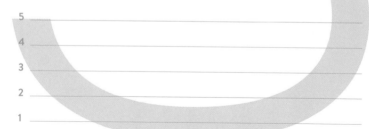

TOP

5

THE TOP FIVE COMMUNITY ACTIVITIES
THAT MAKE ME HAPPY

5 _____

4 _____

3 _____

2 _____

1 _____

Today I did # _____

The most satisfying thing in life is to have been able to give a large part of oneself to others.

Pierre Teilhard de Chardin

What I gave to others today:

_____

_____

_____

DATE: __/__/__

THESE PEOPLE CAUSE HAPPINESS WHEREVER THEY GO:

_____

_____

_____

_____

_____

_____

_____

DATE: __/__/__

THESE PEOPLE CAUSE HAPPINESS WHENEVER THEY GO:

_____

_____

_____

_____

_____

_____

_____

SOME CAUSE
HAPPINESS WHEREVER
THEY GO;
OTHERS WHENEVER
THEY GO.

Oscar Wilde

DATE: __/__/__

HAPPY HOLIDAY!

A holiday I celebrate only occasionally:

_____

_____

_____

Of pleasures those which occur most rarely give the greatest delight.

Epictetus

Today's rare pleasure:

_____

_____

_____

For what should a man live, if not for the pleasures of discourse.

Plato

Today's pleasurable discourse:

_____

_____

_____

The connections we make in the course of a life—maybe that's what heaven is.

Fred Rogers

A heavenly connection I made today:

_____

_____

_____

I wish thee as much reading, as I had

DATE: __/__/__

RATE THE PLEASURE OF WHAT YOU READ TODAY:

POEM

NOVEL

NEWSPAPER

CEREAL BOX

SOMETHING ELSE

pleasure in the
in the writing. ▶ *Francis Quarles*

DATE: __/__/__

RATE THE PLEASURE OF WHAT YOU WROTE TODAY:

BLOG

☆☆☆☆☆

EMAIL

GROCERY LIST

THANK-YOU NOTE

SOMETHING ELSE

_____

How many cares one loses when one decides not to be something but to be someone.

Coco Chanel

Whom I've decided to be:

_____

_____

_____

DATE: __/__/__

TO BE HAPPY, WE MUST NOT BE TOO CONCERNED WITH OTHERS.

Albert Camus

Others I didn't concern myself with today:

_____

_____

_____

DATE: __/__/__

THE DELIGHTS OF MY DAY

Draw a balloon around
at least one.

A CHANCE
ENCOUNTER

SIZZLING
BACON

A SHOOTING
STAR

SILK
UNDERWEAR

THE SMELLS
OF SPRING

A FIREFLY

THE RINGING
OF BELLS

A NEW BOOK BY A
FAVORITE AUTHOR

SNOWFLAKES
ON MY TONGUE

FRESHLY
SQUEEZED JUICE

SOMETHING ELSE

Success to me is having ten honeydew melons, and eating only the top half of each one.

Barbra Streisand

Success to me is:

_____

_____

_____

MUSIC HAS CHARMS TO SOOTHE A SAVAGE BREAST.

William Congreve

This music soothed me today:

_____

_____

_____

EVERYONE SUDDENLY BURST OUT SINGING;

AND I WAS FILLED WITH SUCH DELIGHT

AS PRISONED BIRDS MUST FIND IN FREEDOM,

WINGING WILDLY ACROSS THE WHITE

ORCHARDS AND DARK-GREEN FIELDS;

ON—ON—AND OUT OF SIGHT.

Siegfried Sassoon

Singing that delights me:

_____

_____

_____

How we
are made
for happiness—
how work
Grows play,
adversity a
winning fight!

Robert Browning

DATE: __/__/__

HOW WORK BECAME PLAY TODAY:

_____

_____

_____

_____

_____

_____

_____

DATE: __/__/__

HOW I WON OVER ADVERSITY TODAY:

_____

_____

_____

_____

_____

_____

_____

ONE CANNOT THINK WELL, LOVE WELL, SLEEP WELL, IF ONE HAS NOT DINED WELL.

Virginia Woolf

How I dined well today:

_____

_____

_____

There is no love sincerer than the love of food.

George Bernard Shaw

The foods I love:

_____

_____

_____

LAUGH

AT YOURSELF

How it felt:

_____

_____

_____

Blessed is he who has learned to laugh at himself, for he shall never cease to be entertained.

John Powell

Why I laughed at myself today:

_____

_____

_____

The definition of happiness of the Greeks ... is full use of your powers along lines of excellence. I find, therefore, the Presidency provides some happiness.

John F. Kennedy

How I used my powers for excellence today:

_____

_____

_____

That is happiness: to be dissolved into something complete and great.

Willa Cather

Something complete and great I dissolved into today:

_____

_____

_____

Happiness in the ordinary sense is one is right to aim at it. The through and see those whom

DATE: __/__/__

HOW I CAME THROUGH TODAY:

not what one needs in life, though true satisfaction is to come one loves come through. ▶ *E. M. Forster*

DATE: __/__/__

HOW THOSE I LOVE CAME THROUGH TODAY:

Work is more fun than fun.

Noël Coward

Fun I had at work today:

_____

_____

_____

REGARDLESS OF HOW YOU LOOK AT IT, WE'RE PLAYING A GAME. IT'S A BUSINESS, IT'S OUR JOB, BUT I DON'T THINK YOU CAN DO WELL UNLESS YOU'RE HAVING FUN.

Derek Jeter

How having fun helped me do well at work today:

_____

_____

_____

It made me happy today to receive this invitation:

from:

It made me happy today to give this invitation:

to:

The secret of happiness is to face the fact that the world is horrible, horrible, *horrible*.

Bertrand Russell

The horrible I faced to be happy today:

_____

_____

_____

O, wonderful, wonderful, and most wonderful wonderful! and yet again wonderful, and after that, out of all whooping!

William Shakespeare

An out-of-all whooping today:

_____

_____

_____

DATE: __/__/__

TOP 5

THE TOP FIVE MINDFUL ACTIVITIES
THAT MAKE ME HAPPY

5 _____

4 _____

3 _____

2 _____

1 _____

Today I did # _____

FOR EVERYTHING THAT LIVES IS HOLY, LIFE DELIGHTS IN LIFE.

William Blake

How I delighted in life today:

_____

_____

_____

DATE: __/__/__

VERSE THAT CHEERED ME UP TODAY:

_____

_____

_____

_____

_____

_____

_____

DATE: __/__/__

WISE SAYINGS THAT CHEERED ME UP TODAY:

_____

_____

_____

_____

_____

_____

_____

CHEER'D UP HIMSELF WITH ENDS OF VERSE, AND SAYINGS OF PHILOSOPHERS.

Samuel Butler

It's a helluva start, being able to recognize what makes you happy.

Lucille Ball

I recognized that this makes me happy:

_____

_____

_____

Those who wish to sing always find a song.

Swedish proverb

I found this song today:

_____

_____

_____

When one door of happiness often we look so long at do not see the one that has

DATE: __/__/__

CLOSED DOOR:

closes, another opens; but the closed door that we been opened for us. ▸ Helen Keller

DATE: __/__/__

OPENED DOOR:

Happiness is something that comes into our lives through doors we don't even remember leaving open.

Rose Wilder Lane

The door by which happiness entered my life today:

_____

_____

_____

The measure of my happiness today:

Published in the United States by **CLARKSON POTTER/PUBLISHERS**, an imprint of the
CROWN PUBLISHING GROUP, a division of **PENGUIN RANDOM HOUSE LLC**, New York.

crownpublishing.com
clarksonpotter.com

CLARKSON POTTER is a trademark and **POTTER** with colophon
is a registered trademark of **PENGUIN RANDOM HOUSE LLC**.

ISBN 978-0-451-49680-5

Printed in China

10 9 8 7 6

CONCEIVED AND COMPILED BY Dian G. Smith and Robie Rogge

INTERIOR DESIGN BY woolypear

First Edition